DISCOVER
Canada

by Margaret McNamara

Table of Contents

Introduction

Canada is a country with land. Canada is a country with people. Canada is a country with **geography**.

The Country of Canada

Arctic Ocean

Pacific Ocean

Canada

N
W E
S

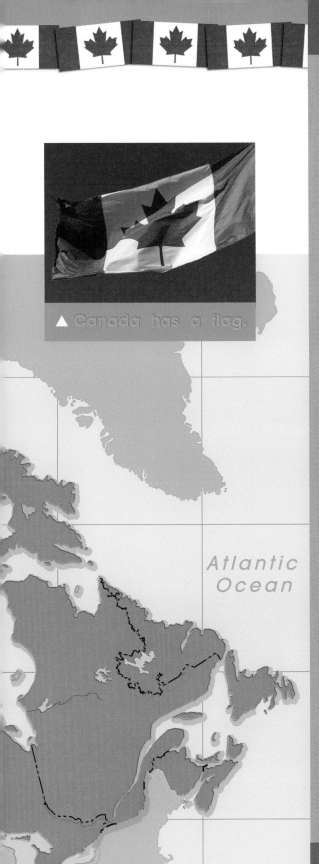

▲ Canada has a flag.

Atlantic
Ocean

Canada

geography

hemisphere

prairies

provinces

territories

See the Glossary
on page 22.

3

Where Is Canada?

Canada is in the Northern **Hemisphere**.

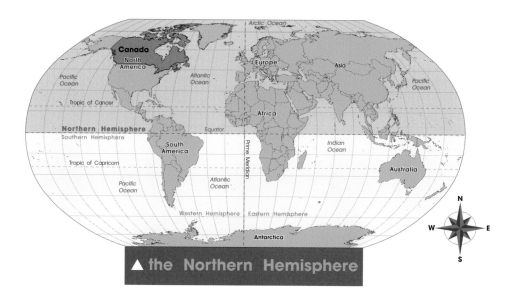

▲ the Northern Hemisphere

Canada is in the Western Hemisphere.

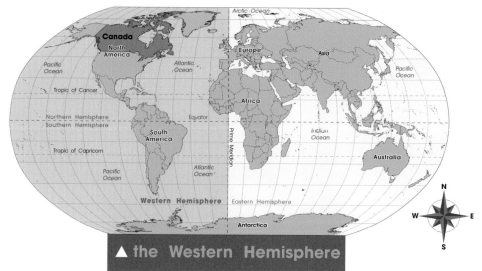

▲ the Western Hemisphere

Canada is in North America.

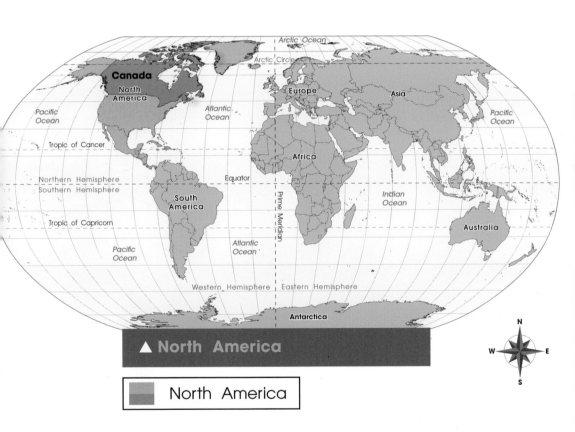

▲ North America

North America

It's a Fact

Canada has land above the Arctic Circle.

5

Canada is near the Pacific Ocean.

▲ the Pacific Ocean

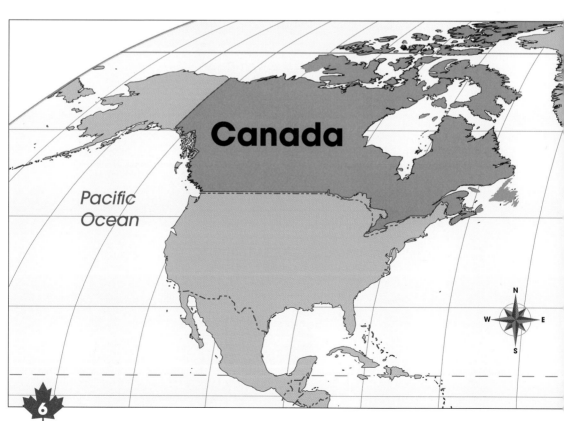

Canada

Pacific
Ocean

Canada is near the Atlantic Ocean.

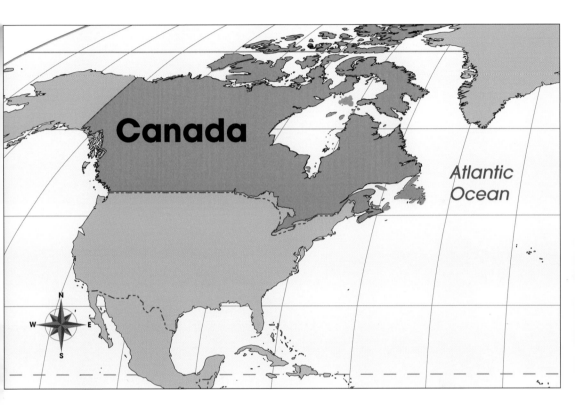

Canada

Atlantic Ocean

▲ the Atlantic Ocean

What Does Canada Have?

Canada has high mountains.

▲These high mountains are in Canada.

Canada has low mountains.

Canada has **prairies**.

▲ This prairie is in Canada.

Canada has ice.

Did You Know?

Canada has polar bears.

▲ **This ice is in Canada.**

Canada has snow.

▲ **This snow is in Canada.** 11

Canada has big lakes.

▲ These big lakes are in Canada.

Canada has small lakes.

▲ These small lakes are in Canada.

Where Are the People?

People are in the **provinces**.

▲ **People live in the provinces.**

It's a Fact

Most people live in the provinces.

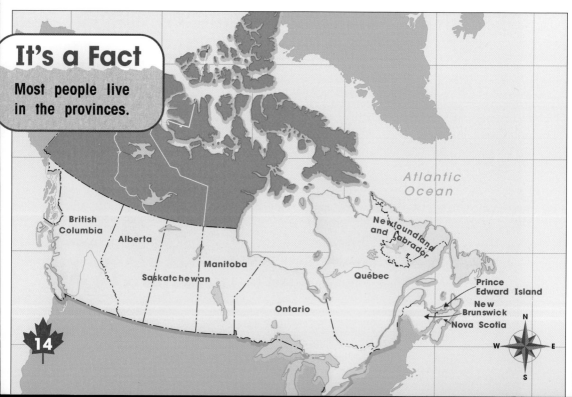

Atlantic Ocean

British Columbia

Alberta

Manitoba

Saskatchewan

Québec

Ontario

Newfoundland and Labrador

Prince Edward Island

New Brunswick

Nova Scotia

People are in the **territories**.

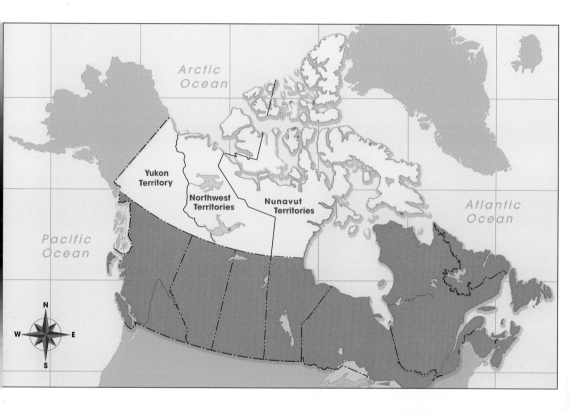

▲ **People live in the territories.**

People are in the cities.

▲ **People live in this city.**

People are in the villages.

ST. JAMES SCHOOL

▲ **People live in this village.**

Conclusion

Canada has places. Canada has people. Canada has geography.

Concept Map

 # Canada

Where Is Canada?

in the Northern Hemisphere

in the Western Hemisphere

in North America

near the Pacific Ocean

near the Atlantic Ocean

What Does Canada Have?

high mountains

low mountains

prairies

ice

snow

big lakes

small lakes

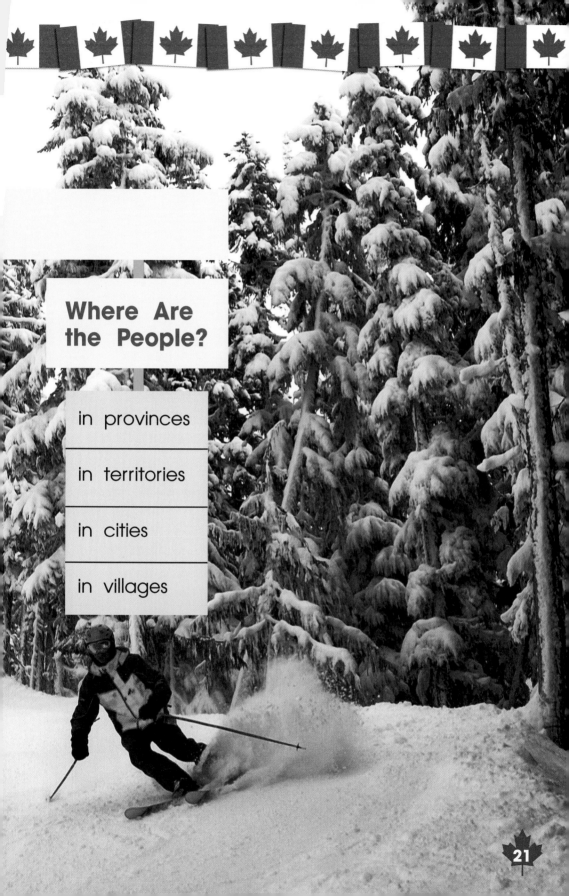

Where Are the People?

in provinces
in territories
in cities
in villages

Glossary

Canada a country

Canada is a country with land.

geography places on Earth; people on Earth

Canada is a country with geography.

hemisphere one half of Earth

Canada is in the Western Hemisphere.

prairies land with very few trees

Canada has prairies.

provinces parts of a country

*People are in the **provinces**.*

territories parts of a country

*People are in the **territories**.*

Index